# Family

/ˈfamɪli,-m(ə)l-/

*noun*

a group consisting of parents and children living together as a unit

"it was where her family lived"

*adjective*

designed to be suitable for children as well as adults

"a family home"

Copyright © 2016

All rights reserved. No part of this publication may be reproduced, stored in a retrieval system or transmitted in any form by any means without the prior permission of the copyright owner. Enquiries should be made to the publisher.

Every effort has been made to ensure that this book is free from error or omissions. However, the Publisher, the Author, the Editor or their respective employees or agents, shall not accept responsibility for injury, loss or damage occasioned to any person acting or refraining from action as a result of material in this book whether or not such injury, loss or damage is in any way due to any negligent act or omission, breach of duty or default on the part of the Publisher, the Author, the Editor, or their respective employees or agents.

The Author, the Publisher, the Editor and their respective employees or agents do not accept any responsibility for the actions of any person - actions which are related in any way to information containted in this book.
The moral right of the author has been asserted.

National Library of Australia Cataloguing-in-Publication entry

Author: Doak, Amy

Title: Family Homes Of The World

ISBN: 9780994412638

Subject: Interior Decoration, Decoration Of Specific Rooms In Residential Buildings

Dewey Number: 747.7

Images by agreement with photographers. Please see page 124 for credits. The Publisher has done its utmost to attribute the copyright holders of all the visual material used. If you nevertheless think that a copyright has been infringed, please contact the Publisher.

Published by:
Of The World Publishing
PO Box 8070
BENDIGO SOUTH LPO  VIC  3550

www.oftheworldbooks.com

# Family Homes
## of the world

# Contents

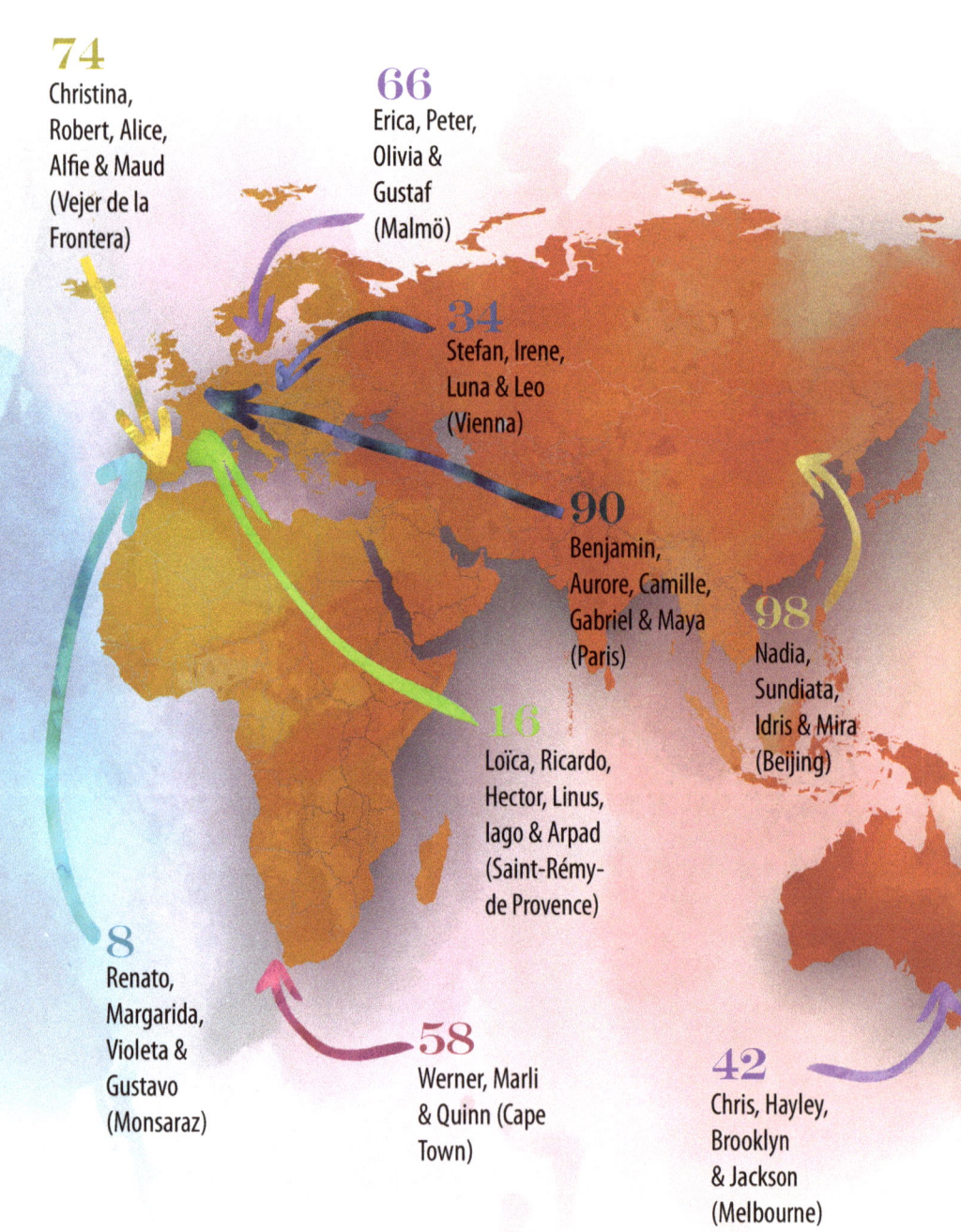

**74** Christina, Robert, Alice, Alfie & Maud (Vejer de la Frontera)

**66** Erica, Peter, Olivia & Gustaf (Malmö)

**34** Stefan, Irene, Luna & Leo (Vienna)

**90** Benjamin, Aurore, Camille, Gabriel & Maya (Paris)

**98** Nadia, Sundiata, Idris & Mira (Beijing)

**16** Loïca, Ricardo, Hector, Linus, Iago & Arpad (Saint-Rémy-de Provence)

**8** Renato, Margarida, Violeta & Gustavo (Monsaraz)

**58** Werner, Marli & Quinn (Cape Town)

**42** Chris, Hayley, Brooklyn & Jackson (Melbourne)

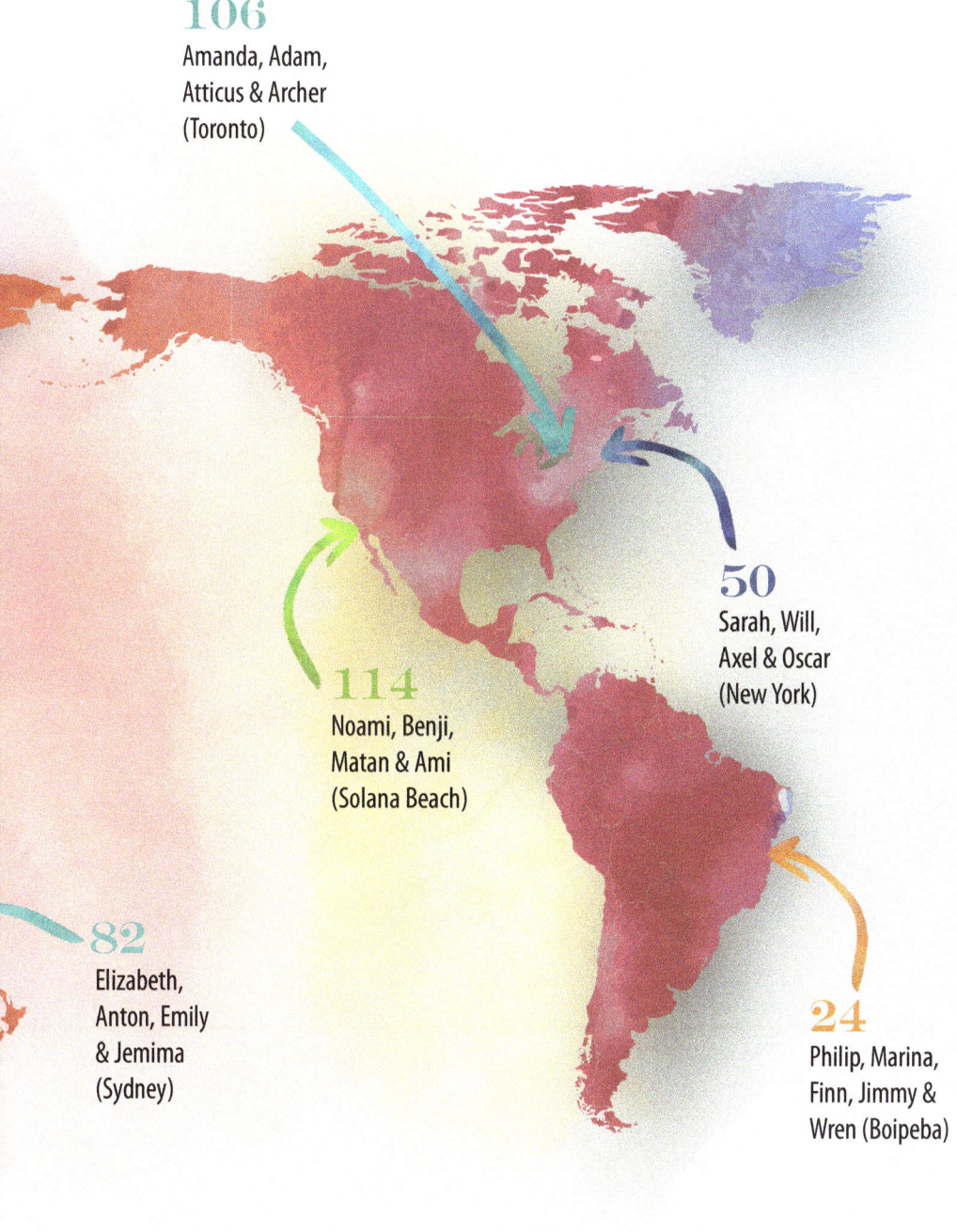

# Introduction

**Something changes in a home when children arrive.**

Of course it's more 'stuff', but it's also something else as well. A warmth, a comfort, an ease that perhaps wasn't there before. I am sure you have strong memories of your childhood home, some wonderful and some not-so-much. The colour of the couch, the touch of the kitchen bench, the sound the curtains made as they closed when the sun was going down, the smell of the one room that you weren't supposed to play in...

They say home is where the heart is and that it's the people who make the home, but the physical space is what creates the memories and what sets the precedent for what you consider to be a home (or not) as you grow.

In this book, we have spoken to families living in 14 homes from 11 different countries around the world. Families with children ranging in age from newborn to 26 years. Families who have found a new country to call home, and others who have found their way back home. Families who are creating memories every day.

The thing I have discovered after speaking to all of these generous people, who have willingly opened up their homes and shared them with you, is that they have more things in common than not. If you are fortunate enough to grow up in a home filled with love, it doesn't matter where you live. All parents want to create a beautiful life for their children, to surround them with things that are special and to create a home that is safe and happy. To give them a childhood they will remember with great fondness, and to set them on a path to adulthood that is filled with confidence, joy and the belief that anything is possible.

In this book, we have beach, country and city homes; some are small and some are large. We have families who speak multiple languages and who have lived in other countries around the globe. Right now though, they are living right where they need to be, and hoping the home they have created will be the one their children will remember fondly for the rest of their lives.

# The Alentejo, Portugal
## Margarida, Renato, Violeta & Gustavo

Portugal's Alentejo region is its largest, covering almost one third of the country. With dry, golden plains, rolling hillsides and lime green vines and the beauty of a rugged coastline, the region offers traditional whitewashed villages, marble towns and medieval cities such as the UNESCO-protected Evora. Cork production, centuries-old farming traditions and local crafts are created here, but the area is really known for its fabulous traditional food. With pork, game, bread, cheese, wine and seafood along the coast, there is plenty to enjoy. The area is equally as idyllic for children with fields of sunflowers, storks nesting on chimneys and rivers and beaches to swim in.

In the centre of the region is one of the most beautiful medieval villages in Portugal, Monsaraz. Around two hours drive from Lisbon, the area is surrounded by vineyards and plenty of nature. Wildflowers abound in the summer and you can enjoy the stars at night.

For Renato and Margarida, who spent their 20s and 30s travelling the world and building their careers, their small corner of Alentejo is heaven on earth.

"We spent a one week holiday here when Violeta was just six months old," Margarida explains. "It was our first holiday to the countryside with our daughter and we loved the silence, the nature, the hot weather. We started dreaming about a life in Alentejo! Chasing the dream meant over 2,500km in a car, weekend after weekend searching for that ideal piece of land."

Violeta has just started school and has been joined by a little brother, Gustavo, who is now 11 months old. The family live in a 1940s flat in Lisbon during the week where Margarida works as a film and advertising producer and Renato as a production manager in fashion. Alentejo is their home on weekends and holidays and they escape to it whenever they can.

"Our heart beats for two homes," says Margarida. The family commissioned their good friend, architect João Favila Menezes, to help them create the home of their dreams. "We wanted to build

something from scratch…something very modern and unique, but also very Alentejano too. A single floor dwelling with white walls, small windows and inside patios is all very Alentejo. We made João a 12-page brief with mood boards, a breakdown of all our wishes and he didn't even read it! He presented us a house without windows and then asked us to look around outdoors and lead us to our rooms via outside patios and let the location decide where things would go. The concept was so unusual and unexpected that we loved it from the beginning. The challenge was then to build it within our tight budget. We had to be a little creative there. We also had the task of creating a garden – and keeping it alive when you have 45-degree Celsius days in summer! We used Teresa Barao from Topiaris and she has been teaching me a lot about plants when my knowledge previously was null!

"We didn't want stairs up or down and we wanted the kids to be able to run inside and outside in the same way. We also knew we wanted a swimming pool and it was important to have that in a visible distance from the house…but not so close that as the kids get older and noisier that we can't rest and relax on the patio."

Margarida and Renato have always loved to travel and that is apparent in much of their home's décor. "We only became a family when I was 38," Margarida says. "For many years before then I spent my free time travelling and collecting. My big passion is interior design and I love fabric and pattern in general, so I have gathered a lot of things along the way. There are so many details in our home that I adore – the wallpaper in our bedroom, the Japanese fabric I bought from Tokyo that has been used for curtains in Violeta's room and covered the old sofas in our kitchen, the old bread bags from my great grandmother that are now pillows in the spare room, the Mexican oil painting…they are all very special to me."

"We love it here. The space, the light, our paintings and furniture and all the little details that we have collected over the years…it's a place that means so much to us all. Here, there is nothing really apart from beautiful nature, shepherds and cattle. At the end of the day there is a really special light that settles over the house, but it is lovely here all day and night."

Margarida believes that having started their family later in life has made them appreciate being parents all the more. After having Violeta, the pair struggled to have another child and after a long and arduous four-and-a-half year adoption process, they were thrilled to welcome Gustavo into their family and make it complete. "It isn't easy to adopt in Portugal so we are very lucky to have him. When you have children, the capacity of loving becomes extensive. Our lives are not centered around ourselves any more and that's a good feeling. You naturally shift your goals to share, to care, to protect and to love someone besides ourselves. We love being a family and we value the principles of individuality, mutual respect and the space that each of us as parents need to be happy too.

"I always knew I would need help in order to be a mother and work as a producer as well. We have a nanny in Lisbon who helps us out when our work schedules are busy. Luckily, that's not every day so I think we have found a good balance between work and being a parent. Renato has just recently sold his café and gone back to a job that means better hours. That's been a blessing as we missed him a lot, but when you have a restaurant those are the hours you must work."

"We are not super woman or super man, but when we are with the children we like to make sure we are 100 per cent with them and it is quality time. The rest of the time, when the 'dream' is not possible, we have to teach them to understand that we have a life outside of being their parents and they have to find their own entertaining moments when we have to work or when we are resting. However, resting doesn't happen very often. We come to Alentejo to enjoy the nature but that also means taking care of it – the pool, the garden, the home, it all takes work but we love it!

"Portugal is indeed a great destination to live. The weather and the geography are definitely a special plus to add quality to our family life here. The people here are warm and friendly and open their home to strangers and it is perhaps this that we miss the most when we travel away. Having this home in the countryside has made our kids love and respect nature, to observe it as the seasons pass by, and that's something wonderful that we can offer them. The Portuguese are very nostalgic and love to complain, but often don't do anything to change the things they don't like. We try to teach our children that if we don't like something, we should change it… because we should always change the world that we touch for the better."

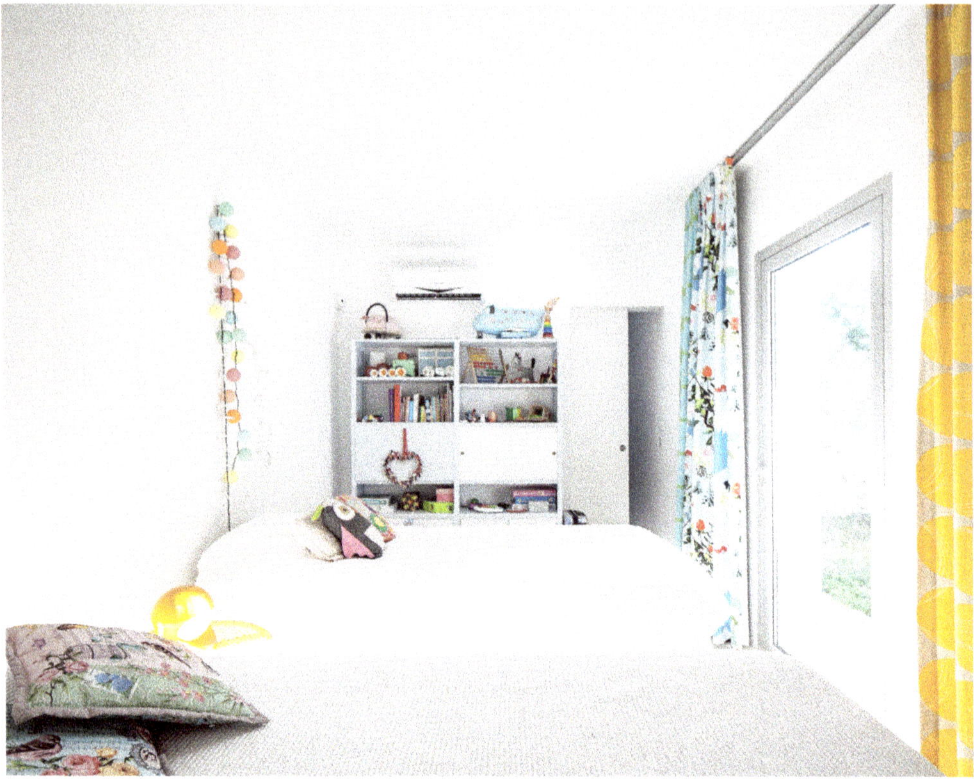

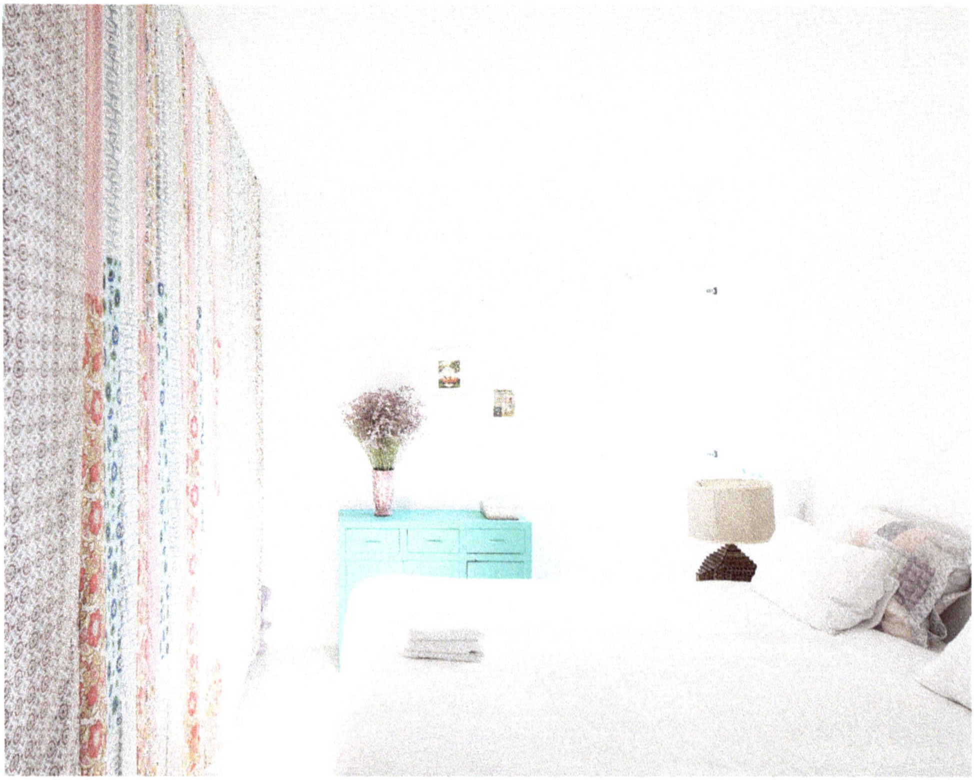

*"We try to teach our children that if we don't like something, we should try to change it... because we should always change the world we touch for the better."*

# Saint-Rémy, France
## Loïca, Ricardo, Hector, Linus, Iago & Arpad

Provence is a geographical region and historical province in southeastern France. It extends from the left of the lower Rhône River on the west, to the Italian border on the east, and is bordered by the Mediterranean Sea on the south. Twelve miles south from the city of Avignon and just north of the Alpilles mountain range is a village called Saint-Rémy-de-Provence.

Saint-Rémy embodies all that is great about the region – art, good living and lots of sunshine. Vincent Van Gogh lived in the village for a time and it's also famous for being the birthplace of Nostradamus. From Roman ruins to picturesque chocolate shops and flower-filled meadows by the river, the town of just over 10,000 residents is like a picture story book.

Ten years ago Loïca and Ricardo were living in Paris when their eldest son, Hector, was born and the couple considered looking for a house where they could spend weekends and holidays as a family. "It was a very Parisian thing," Loïca says. "To find a little house in Provence that you would remodel over time. Instead of that little house, we found a very old, big farm with no electricity and no water. We immediately fell in love with it, but nobody could understand why because it was such a ruin. When our fourth child, Arpad, was born five years ago, we decided it was time to move and live here permanently."

Provence was a region where the family always wanted to put down roots. Loïca's grandmother was born there and, although her family travelled a lot when she was young, Provence was a place they always came for holidays. "There is so much to love here, but I think when a place has the colours, smells and sounds of your childhood you are just attached to it," Loïca smiles. "We have created a simple, family home and it's very easy to enjoy life when you create your own universe. The element I felt the children needed the most was freedom, so the house was pretty much empty when we moved

in and over time we have added some things we love and some things the children love. We definitely applied the 'less is more' theory though. I believe it takes time to figure out what you really want to be surrounded by, and we are always moving furniture about as well!"

A restored farmhouse in Provence doesn't seem like a place that would be filled with lots of plastic toys, and while Loïca concedes that perhaps the children don't have a huge amount, it is perhaps because their idea of play is much more free range. "Unless the boys are building 'houses' with pillows and sheets, they don't really play in their bedrooms," she says. "Living in the country, I find most play happens outdoors and their 'toys' are trees, sticks and mud! When it's really impossible outdoors, the corridor inside is busy and noisy. I store most things in wardrobes and each boy has a pinboard for artwork. We frame the really special pieces. The rest of the things they accumulate – like pottery and strange wooden statues – live in their bedrooms for three months and then they decide if it stays or goes. For the things they keep, I have a 'childhood box' for each child and that is the home of their little treasures."

"Little by little we have definitely started to gather things," Loïca admits. "We travelled from Japan with plenty of robots for (second eldest) Linus, stones from Fiji (they made for heavy luggage) and our parents gave us furniture that we didn't choose but came to like. Everyone thought we needed furniture and so we were given so much...and now I feel like we have too much!"

The boys are all homeschooled and Loïca says although that means the family spends a lot of time at home, they are still all very busy outside the property. "We are out in the afternoons for activities, so I certainly spend a lot of time in the car. We are lucky as there is plenty to do in our area and the boys do horse back riding, gymnastics, ballet, singing and there are amazing art classes at a nearby contemporary art museum. They also enjoy the freedom and all of the adventure that comes with living in the countryside."

"I never realised how much energy you need as a parent," Loïca laughs. "It is 24 hours a day, seven days a week and even though, theoretically, I knew it would be intense, I had no idea I would need such a diverse skill set! Nurse, manager, chef, driver, encyclopedia, party planner, plumber, electrician, kappla expert, Lego wizard...it doesn't end! I do love it though.

"We try to make sure the boys are in bed by 8pm and that's when we enjoy date nights, friends over or just nights reading or talking by the fire. Having four children under 10 is definitely extreme at times though, so when Ricardo and I do have time together we try to avoid talking about logistics! All the practical aspects of life…who goes where, when, how much is it, for how long, repairing the roof, what's for dinner…they are kept out of that special time we have together and that means making fast decisions about things and not making a big deal out of the little things. We are used to it now and it works pretty well for us!"

Despite living in a seemingly-dream location, the family still manage to travel when they can and, like other things in life, it seems Loïca takes a relaxed approach to trips to other countries. "Despite the temptation of taking everything, it's much easier if you travel light. It's important to remember that no matter where you go in the world…they have kids living there. If anything happens, you figure it out with the locals. France is beautiful but to be honest, I don't think any place is the best place in the world. It depends on who you are, and the moment you are in. Any country is best for you at that moment in your life that you are choosing to be there."

For this moment, it seems France is the perfect place for this happy family-of-six. "I love our home, and our life. I love how simple and relaxed it is. I love the end of the day when all six of us end up on Ricardo and my bed and we read before bedtime. I love the evenings in summer when we are all on the terrace quietly listening to music. I adore the warmth, cosiness and love that comes with having four children. Every day is a surprise – when you wake each morning you never really know what the day will bring!"

*"I adore the warmth, cosiness and love that comes with having four children. Every day is a surprise – when you wake each morning you never really know what the day will bring!"*

# Boipeba, Brazil
## Philip, Marina, Finn, Jimmy & Wren

Bahia is one of the 26 states of Brazil and is located in the eastern part of the country on the Atlantic coast. The capital, Salvador, is a jewel-box colonial city with gilded churches, cobblestone streets and lively festivals, set among a backdrop of old stone walls and 16th-century buildings.

Bahia is really known for its 900km of stunning coastline filled with World Heritage-listed sites, deserted beaches, idyllic coastal villages and magical islands. Guide books and locals alike love the feel that Bahia is where South America meets Africa, a wonderful blend of two colourful, creative and musical cultures. One hundred and ten miles south of Salvador is a pristine island called Boipeba, with around 1,600 residents and more than 20km of glorious beaches.

In a small beach village you will find Philip and his family, and although Philip wasn't born and bred in this part of the world, he has certainly found a way to make it home. "The village we live in is populated by Bahian Brazilians, mainly of Afro-Brazilian descent," Philip explains. "It is, materially, quite a poor community but in terms of quality of life and culture, I would say it is quite wealthy. The pace of life is very laid back, most people work in fishing or tourism, so there is always enough to eat and always time to stop and talk with neighbours…and probably have a beer! Culturally, most people are Catholic or Christian, but many still observe the Candomble (West African religion that arrived with the slaves) traditions. This makes for wonderful, colourful ceremonies with incredible dress, dancing and drumming."

Philip and his wife, Marina, found they were spending a lot of time travelling between South America and Europe, but kept missing the summer in both hemispheres, so they decided to move to a place where it was hot all year around. "We had been to the south of Brazil, and we loved it," says Philip. "A friend talked a lot about Bahia so I emailed a few places to rent. One man said, 'well, if you

have kids then you must go to Boipeba Island.' We found a place to rent and went for four months. Marina immediately wanted to live there forever, but I will admit I was a little skeptical. I thought I would go crazy living on a small island after a few months…but those few months went by and before I knew it, I was hooked!"

The family now live in a beautiful home overlooking the perfect blue water of the Atlantic Ocean. Philip admits island life has, in many ways, made life with children both wonderful and challenging. "We work from home (in administration and design) and the kids, like all kids, seem to have lots on…surfing, wood carving, capoeira and Portuguese classes as well as school for the older two. These things take time. Their Capoeira (a combination of dance, acrobatics and marital arts) class is in another village, so we walk with the kids on the horse for one hour to get there, one hour to do the class and then the walk home – so that's three hours for one activity. We definitely need to pace ourselves and adapt to a difference pace here.

"Our lives are very much entwined with our children's lives, particularly living in a small village and working and living in the same space. It's hard to find the balance, especially when work has its demanding moments. I think the key is discipline and organisation, and trying to have fixed work hours so you aren't looking at the computer when you should be with your kids and vice versa. In saying that, you also need to know when to put your hands in the air and admit that sometimes life just happens…and just go surfing when you should be working on spreadsheets!

"A friend of mine once described being a father as an honour – having people who always want to spend time with you no matter what. When your children are small, it's probably the only time in our lives that we get that. It's also rather amazing to be able to teach them something, and even more amazing when you see them learn by themselves."

Philip's home is simple and welcoming, offering beautiful views of the outdoors from many rooms. Many of the items that decorate and furnish the home have been sourced locally. "We found two stores in Salvador that specialise in creating furniture and décor from demolition wood – such as the side table in the sitting room – and these pieces fit really well with the style of the house. However, most of the furniture was made by the two carpenters who built our home. We bought two abandoned fishing boats and dismantled them for the timber. We had some ideas and shared them with Astro and Lito (the carpenters) and they made the most incredible things. I absolutely love the two chairs outside our bedroom. They were made from the ribs of the boat and were incredibly complicated, but are such wonderful pieces. We have also picked up lots of antiques and artisan pieces on our trips exploring Bahia. All of our items are hardy – we have three boys, so delicate soft furnishings are not ideal! They can run a bit wild so it's nice to not worry about things being ruined."

The sitting room and the kitchen are actually two separate buildings linked by an outdoor deck area. "We have large doors that can be opened up to create one big inside-outside living space. It's great because it means the kids can run around and play while we are cooking and preparing meals, and we can still keep an eye on them."

With such a relaxed, beachy vibe in this home, it begs the question: what do you do with all the kids' stuff? "We don't really deal with it, because we don't have it!" laughs Philip. "We live so far from family that we aren't gifted those sort of things and locally, there isn't the same sort of gift culture. We still buy things for the kids, but we try and focus on books, craft things and solidly built toys. Less, but better quality. We do ask people who give them gifts to keep this in mind and we also try to minimise the amount of plastic in the house."

Living in what looks like paradise, it's hard to imagine that this family - who once loved to travel - would want to go anywhere. "Brazil is a wonderful country," Philip agrees. "It certainly has its problems – corruption, lack of organisation – but offsetting these are fantastic people with an incredibly warm nature... people who are very open and kind. We still love to travel, but with children we prefer to go to countries where the culture loves kids. Italy, Spain, Greece, Argentina and Brazil are all great for this and I'm sure there are plenty more. People here make an effort if you have kids. There is a stereotype that Brazilians just love football and partying. Though most people do like football (but no more than in the UK) and like a good time, they also work incredibly hard. Brazil is also vast and it's a country that will surprise anyone who, like I once did, simply equates it with the tropical Amazon.

"Where we live is far enough away from the modern world with all its commercialism and consumerism, but at the same time we are still connected to the Internet so we are not totally cut off. I love the fact we don't have cars here. Just walking, cycling, riding or the occasional boat trip. I like to believe that, although we are far from the modern world, island life is at the same time a microcosm of that world – all the joys, discomforts, challenges and triumphs played out on a smaller scale. Small is beautiful as they say!"

*"A friend of mine once described being a father as an honour - having people who always want to spend time with you, no matter what."*

# Vienna, Austria
## Irene, Stefan, Luna & Leo

Once the centre of the powerful Habsburg monarchy, Vienna is one of the few cities in the world that can boast such imperial grandeur. The capital of Austria, Vienna lies in the country's east on the Danube River. The city was once home to Mozart, Beethoven and Sigmund Freud, and today it has a population over 1.8 million – almost one third of Austria's entire population.

For years Vienna has scored high on livability tests around the globe and it's no wonder: it's beautiful, safe, has an efficient transport system, excellent schools, restaurants and cafés and exciting museums and galleries. In addition to the stunning historic architecture, Vienna is also known for its music, art and culture. The Burgtheater is considered one of the best theatres in the German-speaking world (Vienna is the second-largest German-speaking city in the world, after Berlin), the Vienna Boys' Choir is known throughout the world and, with over 450 balls held in Vienna each year, people travel from all over the globe to attend these spectacular events.

Spanish-born Irene, her husband, Stefan, and two children, Luna and Leo live in the penthouse of a beautiful building in the centre of Vienna and Irene admits they have perhaps found the perfect location in the city.

"We had been living in a suburban area in Zurich – surrounded by fields and cows and a wonderful view to the mountains – but when we decided we wanted to come back to Vienna, we knew we wanted to live in the city centre. We wanted to be near to our jobs (Stefan is an energy consultant and Irene is an architect) and we also wanted to be walking distance to markets and parks. Our last requirement was to have three bedrooms, as I work from home and it was important for me to have a separate office. Oh, and we wanted plenty of light!

"It wasn't easy to find a flat that fulfilled this criteria as most of the apartments that we looked

at were 'old Viennese style'. They had lovely high ceilings and big doors, which we really loved, but they were missing a bedroom or the flat was just too large – often the rooms in these properties are very big. After some searching though, we found it. A 90m2 flat located in an old building in the 6th District of Vienna where the penthouse was completely rebuilt. It was the perfect solution for us.

"We are located between the penthouse and the fifth floor, so we have lovely views of the street and beautiful buildings surrounding us. It's wonderful to feel the atmosphere of the old Viennese buildings, but then to have all the modern comforts of a new home. Light is an absolutely essential element for me – perhaps that is my Spanish heritage – and we've got huge glass windows that create a feeling of openness and space fluidity throughout the whole apartment."

The perfect apartment wasn't just about location and light though… it was also about having the potential to create a family home. "We wanted the whole apartment to have a nice and friendly atmosphere – not just the kids' room. We wanted lots of colourful elements and to ensure the children felt comfortable in every room of the house. When we moved in, we didn't have any knowledge of Maria Montessori and her philosophies, but we arranged our flat in a way that lent itself to the Montessori principles – allowing the kids to have access to the maximum of elements in order to stimulate their independence. We did that intuitively so it was funny that, later on when Luna was starting kindergarten, we chose a Montessori kindergarten. We realised then what we'd done and we had placed our furniture in a similar way to them.

"I do try to avoid commercial elements like cartoon characters on pictures and toys. I definitely choose more timeless decorations like animals or traditional puppets. Some of the 'art' around the house was made by the children. They both really like to paint, so we've used some of their creations to decorate their room and also ours."

"I like to buy in different shops and flea markets when we travel, so there is always something coming into our flat," Irene laughs. "My favourite pieces, without a doubt, are the blankets and handmade cushions. Some were made by my mother, so they have special added value. The colourful blanket in the living room was made by nuns for my father and he gave it to us, so it was a very special gift. Another sentimental piece is the wooden horse swing. It was handmade by Stefan's father, along with other wooden toys, in a little village in the Alps called Bregenzerwald where they live. There is a long tradition there of working with wood and now the children's grandfather is retired, he is doing these things with great interest."

Irene and Stefan's families don't live in Vienna, so this means they have done plenty of travelling over the years. "We visit friends in other countries too, so we travel quite a lot," Irene explains. "We have become experts at travelling with kids! We've learned to travel with as little luggage as possible and, when we can, we make each child responsible for something: their backpack, a kids trolley... They like to feel like they're part of the trip and we find when they've got a little responsibility they tend to enjoy it more and behave better. When Stefan has work commitments I travel alone with the kids and each time it has really been a pleasure. When we all travel together though we make sure the kids are involved in the planning and as well as guided tours, museums or street markets, we also look for a place the kids can play and run, preferably outdoors! This is something they need wherever they are so wherever we go we look for city parks, beaches or fields. Before Stefan and I were married we both did a lot of solo travel and loved it. It's very different when you're travelling with kids, but both are great experiences.

"There is a lot to love about living in Austria. It is so easy to access nature – beautiful mountains and landscapes – and it's a very international community with people living here from all over the world. I also love how easy it is to travel to surrounding countries such as Germany, Italy, Slovenia and Hungary. There are a great variety of things to do with kids here...plenty of museums, concerts and sporting events. The living standard is also very high with good public services, great transport and lots of cultural activities. In saying that, the winters here are long. I don't enjoy the lack of daylight or the cold, grey days. I am definitely made for sunny places!"

With a beautiful home and a love of travel, it sounds like Irene and her family have found the perfect balance. "You get lots of advice before you have children, particularly about how much your life will change. Yes, it's true. Life has changed a lot for us, but we didn't expect how much fun we would have when Luna came into our lives, and then with Leo even more so. Austrian people are very independent but I come from a country where it is all about family. I am still very attached to my parents and siblings and I hope that I can pass those values onto my children. They will have their own life, of course, which is completely natural, but when they are grown I will definitely miss the thousands of hugs and kisses that we give them through the day!"

*"They will have their own lives, of course, but when they are grown I will definitely miss the thousands of kisses and cuddles that we give them through the day!"*

# Melbourne, Australia
## Hayley, Chris, Brooklyn & Jackson

In mid-2015, Melbourne was rated the world's most liveable city for the fifth year running, achieving a near-perfect score on the Economist Intelligence Unit's liveability survey of 140 cities around the globe. Stylish, arty and a great place to find a good coffee in an equally good café, Melbourne is considered Australia's cultural capital. It features goldrush-era architecture and a multicultural population that reflects the city's recent history. Melbourne offers festivals, great restaurants and creative people. It is also renowned for its sporting life – football, cricket, horse racing, Formula One racing and international tennis all take centre stage throughout the year.

To the south east of the city centre is a suburb called Prahran (known to the locals as 'Pran'). With café-lined pavements and stunning Edwardian and Victorian architecture, this leafy corner of the world is known for its great shopping and the famous Greville Street, once the centre of Melbourne's hippy community.

Hayley, who is partner in an accounting firm, and her husband, Chris, who is a carpenter and stay-at-home dad, bought their home in Prahran back in 2010 after looking for a place to call their own for almost three years. "It certainly didn't look like this when we bought it," Hayley laughs. "Chris renovated it all by himself, starting work in November 2013 and completing it by August 2014."

Enjoying their beautiful new home are the couple's sons, Brooklyn and Jackson, and Charli, their kelpie-cross-staffie. "I love where we live," Hayley says. "Everything we could ever need is within walking distance – great parks, a swimming centre, supermarkets, restaurants, markets and cafés."

Finding the perfect home in the perfect area meant Chris and Hayley were finally able to create their dream house. And they had kids in mind when opening up the home to offer a light-filled, open-plan space. "Our kitchen and living area is one great space, which is wonderful because we can watch the kids whilst they play. It also opens out on to an outdoor area. My favourite time of the day is in the

afternoon when the sun shines into that room and we can open the bi-fold doors to let the outdoors in. Nothing is too precious in our home – we want our kids to be able to behave like kids! My eldest son runs or drives his toy car around the kitchen bench for hours on end! The space is great for them to play in and that is really important to us.

"We decked out our home as soon as the renovations were complete. Most of our furniture is from Jardan – the dining table with the marble top and the bench seat are both from there and I absolutely love those pieces! Other favourite items include the shelf on the wall above the dining table that Chris created with leather straps and custom built marble shelves, and the Adam Cullen print on the wall above the fireplace."

So what about all the 'kid stuff' that inevitably comes with small children? "There are advantages having a husband who is a carpenter!" Hayley says. "Chris built an attic space in the roof and we keep a lot of our stuff up there. We rotate toys and equipment every few months, so when Brooklyn is bored with something we just swap it over for something 'new' and we don't have to deal with the clutter. It works well for all of us.

"Life is so much better with kids," Hayley says. "The best part of my day is walking in the door when I come home from work! Brooklyn runs up to me for a hug and a kiss and I am really going to miss that when he gets bigger. It's the sweetest way to arrive home. Chris is so supportive of me and my career but I always put family first so I don't struggle too much with the balance."

Chris and Hayley's philosophy, both in and out of the home, is 'family first' and given growing their family was not an easy task, it is easy to understand why their two boys really are their everything. "As a child, I suffered a rare form of cancer of the uterus and as a result I was unable to carry my own children," Hayley admits. "For many years I wrestled with my own maternal instincts against the possibility of remaining childless or adopting children. After much analysis and deep thought, my husband and I decided to pursue the Californian surrogacy solution (surrogacy is not

an easy process in Australia thanks to many complicated laws that differ state-to-state). Surrogacy is definitely a long process, but we were both so determined that we didn't let things get us down. We just moved through each challenge with the knowledge that we'd have our own children in the end. I have made beautiful connections with both my surrogates. Sarah (who carried Brooklyn) and Amber (who carried Jackson) will forever be a part of our family. They are two selfless human beings who wanted to make a difference in someone's life...and they certainly did that! The process has not just affected us, but also my parents. They always felt they took the ability for me to carry children away but that simply wasn't the case. If they hadn't made those hard choices when I was so young, I wouldn't have survived. Luckily for me, my mum begged the doctor to try and keep my ovaries out of harm's way during my chemo treatment. The doctors gave in to my mother's wishes and hitched the ovaries to my hipbones to keep them out of the way – and told my mother that it probably wouldn't work. Thirty three years later I have two beautiful, biological children thanks to my mother's determination! My ovaries were in perfect working order and enabled us to undergo IVF in the USA to create our children."

Having children via a USA surrogate arrangement has meant lots of travel for this young family. "We've been to the USA five times in the last three years, so you could say we are becoming quite the experts," Hayley laughs. "My number one tip is to try and transition to the time zone of the country you are travelling to the moment you step on the plane – that includes the kids as well. Before you get on a plane, be sure to let the kids move around as much as possible – we always hunt for a play space as soon as we get to an airport. Take your own snacks on the plane – plane snacks aren't always ideal for kids and when they are eating they are sitting still! Travelling with kids is very different to travelling solo or as a couple. For starters, it's not all about you...quite the opposite in fact!"

Despite the family's love of travel, Hayley says Melbourne is definitely the place they love to be the most. "Melbourne is a wonderful place to live and raise a family. It's safe, it's clean and the restaurants are amazing! Plus, we really do have the best coffee in the world. I feel incredibly lucky to have children… we wanted them so bad that, now they are here, we don't even worry about the tough bits! I love holidays, I love days at the park, I love taking them to new places and mostly, I love experiencing life as a family."

"The best part of my day is walking in the door when I come home from work! Brooklyn runs up to me for a hug and a kiss and I am going to miss that so much when he gets bigger."

# New York, USA
## Sarah, Will, Axel & Oscar

In the New York City borough of Brooklyn is the neighbourhood of Williamsburg, home to 113,000 inhabitants and known locally as 'Babyburg' due to its reputation as a hip family hangout. An influential hub of contemporary music, Williamsburg is also considered the place of origin of electroclash music and has a large local hipster culture, a momentous art community and a vibrant nightlife. Connecting to Manhattan's Lower East Side via the Williamsburg Bridge, the neighbourhood has the perfect mix of village atmosphere with city living.

Safe and easy to get around, it's no wonder Williamsburg has become such a favourite of young families over the years. From watching the boats on the waterfront, to the Smorgasburg Street Food Market at snack time, grass rolled out on to the street for weekend picnics on Bedford Avenue and street art-inspired play spaces, playgrounds and hip kids boutiques, you couldn't possibly ask for more.

Will and Sarah have lived in Williamsburg for over a decade, enjoying all it has to offer long before their two children arrived. However, before their first son was born, Sarah – like so many pregnant women before her – took her nesting instinct to a new level. "My husband likes to joke that the nesting instinct is expensive," laughs Sarah. "At the time though, I was itching for more space. Outdoor areas and great light is rare in this city and this apartment had both; floor-to-ceiling windows and two terracaes as well as a shared roof space covered in real grass. We moved in about three weeks before my due date and it felt like a very 'grown up' place to live!"

Sarah and Will couldn't be happier with their home of choice. One subway stop from Manhattan and fantastic views of the Williamsburg Bridge, the location was just the icing on the cake. "The neighbourhood itself is so special," Sarah explains. "Around every corner is a fantastic new restaurant, great street art or a cool little independent business with a fresh take on coffee, ice cream or home

goods. It seems whatever people do here, they do with a passion for craftsmanship and aesthetics, which I love. Our apartment is right in the thick of it all, but it feels like a bit of an oasis, with ginormous bathtubs, rain showers and a good amount of space. It's a quiet, family-oriented building and we're just a few blocks from the riverfront, with great parks and playgrounds, a sense of open space and access to the East River Ferry."

The family love to travel and this has influenced the colour and style of their lovely home. "We have art and other finds from travels to places like India, Morocco and Vietnam," Sarah says. "In fact, we bought our silk lanterns in Ho Chi Minh City and had them shipped back to the States. Will had to go to some very industrial port in New Jersey to get them released from customs. My mother has also sourced some items – she has a great eye for good antiques and flea market finds. I love the boho style of designers like John Derian, India Hicks and John Robshaw who aren't afraid to use a lot of deep, saturated colours and a mashup of wild prints."

The couple's interior design tastes, like travel, has changed over years, as is to be expected with a baby and a toddler in the mix. "In my past, pre-child life, I loved having tablescapes of coffee table books or little objects found on our travels scattered purposefully on various surfaces…those days are long gone! We had some custom cabinetry built to create a wall of bookshelves, so now our tables are object-free and we keep special things up high and out of reach.

"We aren't too precious about anything. Things may look 'designed' but everything is really bomb-proof. Between two cats and two (soon to be three!) little boys, we can't really get worked up about chipped paint or spilled anything. Wood floors are easy to clean and sofa covers can always go in the wash. Our dining room table was actually an old drafting table that was given to us by a friend who is an artist. It came splattered in paint, so I am definitely not worried about messy art projects or ring marks.

"I was a bit of a perfectionist before having kids and, as soon as we had more than one, a lot of that went out the window. I've learned to live with a lot more chaos, though I really have to work to keep my anxiety in check. The first time you visit the ER for gash, it's so traumatic! Weirdly though, you get progressively more calm about the things you can't control. I think that's made me more zen about work, about travel and about the little setbacks you get in any given day."

Despite the madness that comes with small children, Sarah wouldn't have it any other way. "They're hilarious little people. I love seeing their understanding of the world develop. The other day I was explaining to my eldest that birthdays only happen once a year and he said, 'Mama, why are you talking about my ear?' It was a fair point from a three-year-old who hasn't a clue what a year means! We've got a long way to go before they're all grown but when I stumble across a toy race car in my purse or under the bed, rather than feeling annoyed, it just makes me smile. When they're older I will definitely miss those big piles of tiny shoes and funny little totems they find in the park and hide in their pockets."

When it comes to travel, in just a few short years Sarah and Will have discovered a few little things that make seeing the world with kids easier. "Renting a home makes a big difference. We had one trip where the four of us shared a small hotel room at a very nice resort. Trying to feed toddlers in a room with wall-to-wall carpet and store their food in a mini-fridge can be frustrating, as is having the lights off so that they can sleep and it's barely 8pm. We had thought having a daily cleaning service would be great, but they always seemed to arrive when it was naptime. When in doubt, have fold-up strollers for everyone! We were recently in Europe with our 15-month-old and almost three-year-old, and while the older one walked for a bit, it was nice to have the option to contain him at the airport and at museums, and also for naps. Can you put an eight-year-old in a stroller? I would if I could!"

At the end of the day though, there is no place like home. "New York is certainly one of the more vibrant, open, international places on earth. I think people may imagine that New York is a tough place to visit with kids but we find it a really child-friendly place to live," Sarah says. "Sunsets over the city are great, especially in the winter. I love seeing the trains rumbling over the Williamsburg Bridge in the distance and things like sea planes, helicopters and flocks of sea birds. It's like living in a Richard Scarry book."

*If you're keen to learn more about this vibrant and family-friendly part of the world, Sarah blogs about family and city life at www.williamsburgbaby.com*

"New York is certainly one of the more vibrant, international places on earth. I love seeing the trains rumbling over the Williamsburg Bridge and things like sea planes, helicopters and flocks of sea birds. It's like living in a Richard Scarry book."

# Cape Town, South Africa
## Marli, Werner & Quinn

Cape Town is the third most populous urban area in South Africa (after Johannesburg and the Durban area) and the tenth most populous city in Africa with over 3.7 million residents. The stunning city has been named one of the top five Blue Skies Cities in the world and with average temperatures ranging from 17 degrees Celsius in the middle of Winter to a lovely 26 in the height of summer, it's practically perfect all year round.

A city of determined pioneers, Cape Town is proudly multicultural with Christian, Jewish, Muslim, Hindu and traditional African beliefs co-existing peacefully. From the beauty of Table Mountain National Park through to the up-and-coming creative culture of the city with its Cape Dutch architecture and the amazing coastal roads, Cape Town certainly has many stories to tell.

Marli, her husband, Werner and daughter, Quinn, are passionate Capetonians and despite their love of travel, they adore their home country more than anywhere they've been. "Werner and I are fortunate to have travelled the world," Marli admits. "We've even lived on other continents, but we are very passionate about South Africa. There are big stereotypes about our country and many are true and hard to challenge. Vast social inequalities do exist and unacceptably high crime statistics are one sad result of that. We really urge people to come and see the flip-side of the coin though – a country that acknowledges it has far to go, people who are strong and resilient but never hard-hearted. Even while some people live in poverty and great need, you will struggle to find a warmer welcome. We want to be here and we want to be part of the change, so we believe that everyone should put South Africa at the top of their travel list. The place is magic."

Marli and Werner's character-filled cottage is as warm and inviting as the family itself and Marli's love of her little home is as strong as that of her country. "When Werner and I were looking to buy, I

actually fell in love with a much more modern home, but we missed out on it. I'd almost given up on finding somewhere special but Werner persevered and came across this house. The night we came to look at it for the first time it was lit up with candles, all gleaming and warm. The previous owners were a Dutch couple of a similar age to us and we got along famously. We had hardly even looked at the house in detail, but it just felt so right!

The unique cottage even features a magnificent vine growing through the hallway. "All the homes in our street originally had these vines growing just outside the outer walls in the back garden," Marli says. "As people renovated, the vines were often sacrificed. Whoever worked on our house decided to build around the plant! So, the roots and trunk are inside, but the bulk of the vine is outside and keep us nice and shaded in summer.

"Our home is compact and contained, but more than spacious enough for the three of us. We have friends and guests staying over more often than not – our courtyard parties have become legendary. We have amazing parks, museums, the hippest coffee shops and restaurants, gyms and grocery shopping, all right on our doorstep. The winelands, the ocean, world class shopping and dining… they're all within 20 minutes drive!"

Perfect location aside, there is much more to life in Cape Town that Marli and Werner adore. Little by little they have been making changes to the cottage and really making the space their own. "Our house is definitely a work-in-progress!" Marli laughs. "Every few years I get a bee in my bonnet to do something new, but then we weigh up the costs of renovating versus travel and we always end up going somewhere. So, we are very lucky to have borrowed, found and received some beautiful pieces, so it all seems to work well in the end. I love light and heat and we get most of it in the afternoon from the courtyard side of the house. Quinn can usually be found in the courtyard messing about with water or having a tea party with her dolls. We love the inside-out living around the courtyard and in winter I placate myself by turning on the lights and lighting a roaring fire in the lounge."

Initially, Marli and Werner brought items home out of love, but a smaller space has meant that everything has purpose. "The chandelier light fitting in the dining room was a Valentine's Day gift from Werner when we were engaged," Marli says. "We were renting an industrial loft-style apartment at the time and had absolutely no idea where it would go! A Perspex display table that houses Quinn's paintings was our first impulsive art purchase from the Youngblood Gallery in Bree Street on their opening night. I am sure that Nadine Froneman, the artist, wouldn't have imagined that it would one day house baby scribbles! There is nothing 'precious' in our home – things have to have a pleasing form and a specific function... actually, multiple functions ideally. So, cabinets become children's stoves, rubber vases become bath toys and benches are balancing beams."

It's not just their inquisitive toddler who has helped in re-shaping their home – Marli and Werner both balance unique careers that require time and space. "Werner has just recently started working for himself and as an entrepreneur in plastics, Uber and app development, he needs a flexible space to focus, get inspired, meet likeminded folk and get administrative work done. I am a self-confessed neat freak, so we are still working out his new space!"

Marli who, when she is not looking after Quinn, works as a model and actress, admits the most important thing when it comes to finding balance is being prepared to ask for help. "Involve grandparents, aunts, uncles, grown-up cousins or any broody friends you may have! People may be happy to be involved, but they won't always ask so I think it's important to equip your loved ones with a level of comfort and confidence so they're happy to help out. If you're not lucky enough to have or live near a natural support structure, then save up and purchase some free time! Here in South Africa, we are blessed with great helpers who are very affordable – there is absolutely no reason to struggle on alone. Quinn has had a part-time nanny since she was nine months old and that's been an absolute lifesaver. You can overcome guilty feelings of leaving your precious ones with other folk by remembering your baby wants you to be happy too. I am definitely more patient and more fun when I've had some time for me!

"As Quinn has grown from baby to toddler, I've also realised that if we are having fun, then she probably is too, so we look to do things we all enjoy. I am so excited to show Quinn the world, but the simple things are wonderful too. Baking cookies, kicking up leaves, splashing in puddles. I am sure at each different stage with Quinn the things that are fun (and not so fun!) will also be different, but I know already that when she is grown I will miss having her near, knowing all about her day and how it went and knowing that she is happy and safe. For now, we will just enjoy her passion for pink princesses – despite our best attempts at instilling ideas of gender neutrality and feminism – and watching as she rules our home with her magic wand."

"We are very passionate about South Africa. We want to be here, we want to be part of the change and we believe that everyone should put South Africa at the top of their travel list."

# Malmö, Sweden
## Erica, Peter, Olivia & Gustaf

In southern Sweden and close to the Swedish Riviera, Malmö is Sweden's third largest city. With a population of almost 700,000 Malmö is linked to Copenhagen via the Oresund Bridge, meaning that Denmark's capital is just 40-minutes drive away. With a progressive, contemporary feel, Malmö is home to Scandinavia's tallest building, beautiful parks, modern museums and delicious cuisine. Over 150 different nationalities live together peacefully in what is Sweden's most multicultural metropolis and the city is also known throughout the world for its innovation.

Voted the sixth most bicycle-friendly city in the world, the Malmö University opened in 1998, truly establishing the city as a wonderful place to raise a young family. Gamla Staden (Old Town) is the city's heart and is encircled by a canal with a castle, Malmöhus Slott, situated in a leafy park at the western end. The castle is a firm family favourite and the harbourside is also home to a fairytale themed playground for both the young and young at heart.

For American-born, Erica, her Swedish husband Peter and their two children, creating a home was all about living in harmony with one another. "Before we moved in, we worked with a New York-based Feng Shui consultant, Reiko, to help us determine how to arrange our rooms, decide on which colours to use throughout the house and how to improve the general 'flow' of the place," Erica explains. "Over the years, we've continued to gain insights and get advice, and our advisor has very much become our beloved friend. In all likelihood, we will probably always be making changes – we see our home as an extension of our own lives. Hopefully, just like our home, we will continue to grow in understanding over the years and change to become our best selves. Right now, our home is all about being relaxed and happy."

Erica has worked as a teacher for almost 20 years, which has also influenced her thinking, particularly when it comes to children's rooms. "We wanted our children to have spaces to create,

explore and read and also to have a space that can be a little untidy at times. It is, however, important for bedrooms to be a restorative place, so we make sure the kids don't have many toys in their rooms. The room next to our kitchen is used as a playroom, but as their needs and interests have evolved, we are in the process of transforming this space into more of a games room. Having their screen time in such a public place allows us to monitor what's going on and therefore keep them a little safer from the negative influences of the online world. Using the space as a family to play board games and other more traditional games has also been wonderful as it gives our children a sense of pride that their interests are important to the family as a whole.

"We've been going through a bit of a revolution about 'stuff' actually," Erica concedes. "A friend at work gave me the book, *The Life Changing Magic Of Tidying Up* by Marie Kondo and it's a slow process, but we've been getting there. I've realized that all those tried and true toys, like wooden blocks, are the things the kids continue to go back to. With everything else, I am trying to be responsible and we've found a great second hand children's clothes and toys place. The children sell what they don't really want or need, or what they've grown out of, and they keep the money for something special – like a holiday splurge. The special pieces that are really loved or valued go to another family that we are good friends with who have younger children. I still haven't figured out a way to manage the stuffed animals though!"

Given the dark and long Scandinavian winters that Malmö experiences, Erica has found both colour, and special pieces in the home, can make all the difference to the mood. "Colour is really important to me, those dark winters can be difficult. One of the ways I like to introduce colour is through art. I usually go to the online site www.newbloodart.com to find work from up and coming artists. It supports real artists and already some of the pieces we've bought have increased in value. Another one of my favourite pieces in the home is a round, gilded cast iron hanging lamp. I bought it at a second hand store in Milan when I was having a weekend away with one of my oldest and closest friends. It casts a magical pattern of light against the walls around it and it always reminds me of my dear friend. The pieces we appreciate and enjoy the most are those we've found along the way to meet a specific need. Now, before I buy anything I think of Reiko who always asks me, 'OK...but where will it go?'"

When it comes to parenting, much like with her home, Erica takes a philosophical view. "Kids are the best – when they're around there's almost always a positive energy. However, we didn't realize that parenting could be so tiring! We're always looking for the strength, the time, the energy and the money to bake those cupcakes, make that 'jet pack out of the old cola cans' or buy the new bike. Happily, our children's gratitude and love refuels us time and time again, though. Finding the perfect balance is probably impossible, so I see life more as a seesaw where sometimes one aspect of your life gets more priority, and then another aspect will. It seems that women especially are hard on themselves – aiming to be all things to all people at all times. When our children were smaller, I remember Peter casually commenting that maybe our four-year-old didn't have to be on the soccer team. In that moment, the problem was solved. Since then, I try really hard to take the 'long view' picture as often as possible. We will miss the endless laughs and all their funny little jokes and stories when they're grown. I've been trying to write it all down in a book for them, but it's like holding a tin cup under a waterfall!"

Erica and Peter first met in a restaurant in Copenhagen and since meeting they've lived both in Copenhagen and New York before moving to Sweden. "We sometimes dream about living in sunny California," Erica admits. "Although, Sweden, and Scandinavia in general, is a lovely, family-focused place. A lot of planning and government sponsored programs help make this part of the world very livable. Through the support of various companies – either via their own initiatives or the strength of national unions – employees have a fantastic work/life balance. For both men and women. All of these forces working together allow for paid child sick leave, mandatory vacation days, maternity and paternity leave, free organic hot lunches for school children and 37-hour work weeks!

"Creating a cozy and welcoming environment is also very important here. Most families have big tables and candles everywhere as most entertaining is done at home and is centered around food. The lightness in summer and the darkness in winter definitely influences people's moods and also allows for lots of seasonal celebrations. There is also a real focus on things being authentic. Life is celebrated for its flaws and people accept and expect that life can get messy sometimes, which helps set a more realistic and achievable reality. It allows us to forgive ourselves and have more happiness. As a family, we have made a conscious decision about what we have around us because we want our atmosphere to reflect joy and happiness. When we are with our little family, and when we are in our home, it feels harmonious and that is just what we hope for."

*"As a family, we have made a conscious decision about what we have around us because we want our atmosphere to reflect joy and happiness."*

# Vejer, Spain
## Christina, Robert, Alice, Alfie & Maude

A rocky, sun-baked region on the south coast of Spain, Andalucia embodies much of what the world considers Spanish: flamenco, tapas, matadors and white-washed villages. The most populated area in Spain, Andalucia is home to over 8 million people and the region boasts approximately 300 sunny days a year.

One and a half hours drive from Andalucia's capital, Seville, and 40 minutes from the popular tourist town of Cadiz, is a gorgeous little village off the beaten track. Vejer de la Frontera is a stunning white town, clinging to the mountains and overlooking the Cape of Trafalgar and its glorious beaches. An authentic Spanish village with a dash of Moorish influence, Vejer de la Frontera is charming and traditional with palm trees in cobbled squares, tapas bars and narrow winding streets to explore.

The television is flooded with 'Escape To...' type shows with retired Brits living the dream by taking up a second home in the warmth of the Spanish countryside. One clever family made the choice to undertake this lifestyle change when their youngest child was just one year old. Now, 15 years on, they love it just as much and their children have been able to call both Spain and the UK 'home'. "We used to rent houses when we went on holidays," explains Christina. "Having three children it was just too expensive to stay in hotels. Fed up with cheap furniture, broken beds and dirty crockery, we decided to get a place of our own that we could visit every holiday. We absolutely loved the area and it was a place we wanted to explore further, so having a base in Andalucia was the perfect solution. To be able to afford maintenance on the property, we let friends use it to help pay the upkeep.

"It really has become a home away from home. We go for several weeks, several times a year and it's so lovely to stay somewhere beautiful and special with all the comforts of home," Christina says. "The house works for adults and children because it's not too perfect that they can't feel comfortable...but it's tidy enough that they are living in an orderly fashion and don't just throw their

stuff anywhere. We have definitely found that other people respect your house when it looks and feels like a home. It's the perfect harmony of not living in a show house, but living with admiration of your space."

This rambling, atmospheric home is easy to admire – it's full of rustic, romantic character from the cobble stone floors to the studded front door, beamed ceilings and shaded, bougainvillea-filled garden. "It's very old, from the 15th century, with an old, steep staircase and we knew we needed to make it safe for children, but we also didn't want to ruin the feel of the property. With the hard floors, it isn't the most relaxing house for very young toddlers…and the kids have all grown up with their fair share of accidents! They've always loved the house though - our children and visiting kids. We added a corner bed area outside that the kids lie in during the heat of the day, shaded by the bougainvillea. At the other end of the garden is a hammock, so we make up for the lack of soft carpets with other incredibly comfortable areas.

"I think lunchtime is my favourite time of the day when we are in Spain. In London everyone is busy, but here we are all together. Sitting in the courtyard patio as a family and eating local fresh fish and salad – it's perfect."

Although Christina and her family are not in Spain every day of the year, they have still managed to create a beautiful, warm and inviting home. "We have been here 15 years now and we've gathered many pieces over the years. I am constantly upgrading, changing and replacing things. I think my favourite items are the Mexican tin votives and artifacts that I bought in Mexico, and the beautiful fabrics from Morocco. We've also put the kids artwork in frames, and they blend in perfectly with the real artists' works that we have. I still frame them professionally, even though they are children's art. We keep toys and other items in nice-looking woven baskets which suits the style and look of the house – although I always ensure there is storage space under the beds for extra things."

Christina works as a photographer and Robert is a writer and radio broadcaster and even with three children in tow, they have found ways to travel over the years. "Robert worked as a travel writer for many years," Christina says. "Our holidays were always filled with culture, good food and seeing new places. We never stay still! Travelling with children is definitely a challenge, getting everyone on time to eat, meet or even do the same things, but we are used to it now and the kids learn to just go with our plans. Usually we discuss the night before what we are aiming to do. When we travel without kids, it's very different – we have a siesta back in our room pretending we are young lovers. We probably start a little earlier without children too, getting out to see more museums and sights, whereas with kids we limit those visits so as not to bore them."

Now that Christina and Robert's eldest child is 26, they are looking forward to enjoying holidays with grandchildren and having a bigger brood calling Vejer de la Frontera home. "Family life is chaotic, never quiet," Christina admits. "It's also exciting and adventurous. Each day brings something different. Now the children are older, you would think they would be more self-sufficient, but they still call for advice, help or just a chat. It's wonderful to feel needed and useful. When they are all out, we wonder what to do with ourselves! The house is empty and stays tidy, and the fridge remains full, which I never imagined would be a bad thing, so we try to keep our family time with weekly dinners.

"We still always have family holidays together – sometimes the kids bring friends, but we always try to have one holiday when it's just the five of us and we can argue, debate and laugh together. Even though Alice is no longer living at home, we still like to go out to dinner as a family, or even a Sunday roast at home. I think that you have to include your kids in your adult pastimes and enjoyment and so we try to go somewhere new and different to stimulate our minds."

Despite the years passing and busy times ahead, family life in Spain is a tradition that will continue for many years to come for this tight-knit family. "We love Spain for its laid back pace and its culture and traditions. The climate is near perfect and the sea is forever changing and beckoning. Some people say they feel forced to go on holiday, but we look forward to going, year after year!"

*"We have definitely found that other people respect your house when it looks and feels like a home. It's the perfect harmony of not living in a show space, but living with admiration of your space."*

# Sydney, Australia
## Elizabeth, Anton, Emily & Jemima

The capital of New South Wales and one of Australia's largest cities, Sydney is known for its Opera House and Harbour Bridge, located at the waterside hubs of Darling Harbour and Circular Quay. The first British settlers arrived here in 1788 to found Sydney as a penal colony, the first European settlement in Australia. Despite earlier structures being built to a bare minimum of standards, the city now has World Heritage listed buildings and dozen of Commonwealth Heritage listings.

There are over 1.5 million dwellings in Sydney and terrace houses, Federation homes and workers cottages in various suburbs all create a landscape that is uniquely Sydney and indicative of the dynamic history that Australia has had in a short time. Also known for its glorious beaches, beautiful weather, fabulous parks and open public spaces, Sydney is usually the first stop on the tourist map when people visit Australia.

Residing in one of those iconic terrace houses in the Sydney suburb of Paddington is Elizabeth, Anton and their two young daughters. "My husband and I moved here one year after we were married, about a year before Emily arrived," Elizabeth says. "We fell in love with it at first sight – the classic Paddington terrace features, pressed ceilings, arched hall, entry ways and exposed floor boards. It was flooded with natural light, still had the original doors and windows and the sun-soaked terrace off the kitchen offered views over Rushcutters Bay."

It was this character and beauty that won them over, and still impresses the young family today. Despite the age of the home, modern touches have provided the family with everything they could need. "Our living areas are pretty small but we've found that great built-in joinery works well in small spaces. We had our living room sideboard custom designed and it's been an absolute lifesaver when it comes to adding more storage to the room."

Just like the structure of the home, the contents are the perfect blend of old and new. "Most of our furniture has been handed down to us from family members over the years," Elizabeth admits.

"There are a few things we've added – pretty and practical pieces like the great belly baskets from Olli Ella that house all the toys. Most of all though, I love the artwork we've accumulated. A big beautiful abstract by local artist, Michelle Edinger, and my beloved Australian landscapes which were painted by my talented step brother, James Kearns. I've also found some really cute pieces from Etsy for the girls' room. It's all a bit eclectic but it works for us…and I am looking forward to justifying the investment in new furniture once the girls grow older and are a little more responsible!"

Having small children has impacted the décor to a degree…not that you'd realise it when you look at the beautiful light and bright space the family has created. "I think keeping a bit of a 'nothing is too precious' policy has worked well for us while the girls are young. I would love nothing more than a white couch, but it's just not practical with babies. I try to keep things simple and attempting to keep things tidy goes a long way towards a calm and happy household."

The girls share a room and Elizabeth says that the transition to room sharing was far easier than she anticipated. "We didn't move them into the same room until Emily was out of a cot and Jemima was sleeping through the night. The girls are close together in age (20 months) and we moved them in together when Jemima was a little over 12 months old. I am surprised at how little they've disrupted each other! I think they really like sharing a room now and sleeping close to one another."

Elizabeth and Anton both work in the city in law and finance and their home in Paddington is just a 20-minute commute. "Living close to work was really important to both of us – it means we get to spend more time with the kids. We also love the outdoors and the beach, so being close to Bondi and our favourite harbor beaches, Redleaf Pool and Camp Cove, is lots of fun. We love Rushcutters Bay Park and all our local Five Ways cafés and shops. Paddington is a very close-knit community…the houses are attached so it helps if you know your neighbours well and enjoy their company!"

Despite choosing a suburb that helps the family work/life balance, Elizabeth admits that can still be a challenge. "I'm still figuring that one out," she laughs. "I think the key is to try and carve out some time for yourself. Exercise is pretty important to my sanity and I always feel better if I get out of the house and go for a walk or a swim. Spending time with friends is so rejuvenating as well – laughing and getting perspective is very important."

Taking time out and spending time quality together is something Elizabeth says the family tries to do regularly. "We love travel and wish that we could do more of it. Australia is a long way from the rest of the world though, and travel is difficult because of the flights. These days, most of our travel is domestic. We spend a lot of time at Avoca, which is a sleepy little beach town just north of Sydney. It's our happy place and our girls just love it. My husband has spent every summer there since he was born and I hope our girls will be able to enjoy the same.

"I definitely think it's hard to beat Sydney in terms of livability. It's one of the best cities in the world to bring up kids. The natural beauty of the place – the beaches, the parks and the stunning harbor – is second to none. We feel so blessed to be able to share it with our children and have them call it home. To be honest though, we became a family in this house and really, that's what makes it home. That, and all of the memories that we've amassed since we've been here.

"When they're older, I will miss the chaos...but I will also miss the giggles and the hugs. I love the evenings – when the girls are fed and bathed and ready for bed. I adore the cuddles and reading to them. It's the greatest gift, the time we spend together. One day, their evenings will be filled with homework, talking to friends and social media and they won't need me to tuck them in. So, for now, we read stories together and wind down before lights out. It's a beautiful, peaceful time in our house and it makes me feel incredibly grateful for all that we have."

"We feel so blessed to call Sydney our home. To be honest though, we became a family in this house and really, that's what makes it home."

# Paris, France
## Benjamin, Aurore, Camille, Gabriel & Maya

Paris, the capital of France, is known as a global centre for art, fashion, gastronomy and culture. Its picturesque 19th-century city cityscape is criss-crossed by wide boulevards and the River Seine. With a population of over 12 million (and over two million of those residents living in the very centre of the city), the City of Lights is also known for its quaint alleyways and many stunning apartments and buildings.

Paris is divided into 20 arrondissements, or administrative districts, and each has a life and flavour all of its own. In the area where the 5th, 6th, 13th and 14th arrondissements meet, you will find many houses and lofts that are classified as 'monuments historiques' and it's this history that sets the scene for the creative, historic and bohemian feel of the neighbourhood. With the Paris Catacombs, Montparnasse and the Luxenbourg Gardens only a stone's throw away, this is the view of Paris that tourists dream of discovering.

Benjamin, Aurore and their family have been living in their light and open Parisian loft home since just after their youngest child, daughter Maya, was born. "We bought the loft three years ago," Benjamin says. "At the time, we were living in a house that we had just renovated. Although it was a beautiful home and just five minutes' walk from Paris it was, as we say here '*de l'autre côté du périphérique*'... but not in '*Paris intra muros*'. Both Aurore and I were very nostalgic for our daily life in Paris and the suburb we were in was just too quiet for us. Paris isn't like London or New York — there is a very big difference in the lifestyle between Paris *intra muros* and Paris *extra muros*, and we wanted our children to grow up in the Paris that we love right now...not the one that we might love 10 years from now. So, we sold our house to come back to Paris and we were so lucky to find this loft in the district '*quartier*' where I lived all my childhood and did my studies, and where all my family still live."

In one of the most creative areas of the city, Benjamin and Aurore found a stunning loft apartment filled with history and fell in love with it immediately. "The '*Cité verte*' is an artist's cité," explains Benjamin. "Many artists, comedians, architects and cinema producers live here and it has

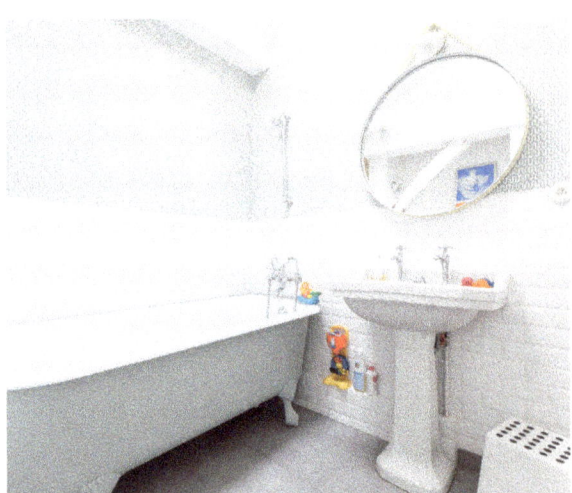

a real authentic Parisian atmosphere. We bought the loft from César's daughter. César (the famous French sculptor) bought it years ago and his daughter had taken over the place. When we visited the loft for the first time, it was full of his souvenirs — sculptures, working masks, drawings for his grandchildren — it was very romantic in spite of the renovation it needed. We kept the big library he designed but we needed to make a lot of changes. It still has a real bohemian atmosphere though."

The loft has four sets of stairs and Benjamin and Aurore have dedicated two sets for the parents, and two sets for the children, in an attempt to give everyone some space in the large, open area. "Our 'survival zone' is the living room," Benjamin laughs. "So, we try to keep some order both there and also where I work... but the rest of the house I can let you imagine!"

Despite living with three small children, the family has incorporated many classic and historic pieces in to the décor of the home and the eclectic mix suits the space perfectly. "We have gathered them over the years," Benjamin says of the unique pieces in the family home. "We have furniture from Louis XIV to Charles Eames and sculptures, paintings or photos from XIX century (family portraits) to today (contemporary photographers). Our favourites are ceramics created by our good friend Gregoire Scalabre, and also serigraphies from new realist artists such as Klasen and Monory. We found the Monory serigraphies in Marché Paul Bert, the flea market in Saint Ouen. It's still a place where you can find unique pieces and they're not as expensive as you might imagine. The décor of our home is a reflection of our past and present life. Each piece is a part of our family culture. For instance, the bronze sculpture of the dog...it's the same as the dog of Aurore's great grandfather (who was both a banker and sculptor).

"It's a wonderful home — the light and silence — it offers plenty of inspiration. When the children are home from school, the open kitchen works really well for the family. We have a big dining table where the boys do their homework while we finish our work for the day, or we prepare dinner. We love having a big space where we can focus on our personal projects but where we are also very much all together."

Despite the cultural and creative lifestyle the family enjoy, there is still time for all of the adventures that young families everywhere seem to have. "I work from home and Aurore has a little studio and showroom between Pigalle and Montemartre. With the children, we try to show them all of Paris and not just '*Paris rive gauche*' where we live. Camille and Gabriel were born in Bastille, where we had our first loft, so we are still very connected to eastern and northern Paris. Our weekends are short though as the boys play rugby and I am a coach in their club. If Aurore and I go out we prefer to do so during the week so that the weekend is dedicated to the children. Aurore and I often like to meet for lunch, or perhaps visit an exhibition, when the children are in school."

Benjamin admits that one of the lovely things about being a parent is that your children keep you young. "You still feel like a child when you are with them. Children have this wonderful natural good mood, and such an open mind. They are a permanent source of happiness and this is something that we try to preserve."

The family enjoys travel, and as well as family trips, Benjamin or Aurore even try to get away with one or two children at a time so both the adults and children are able to enjoy some special, one on one time. It seems though, that for this family, Paris will always be home. "There are many stereotypes about Parisians…that Parisians are not open minded, or they're pretentious…or that the city is a museum. However, Paris is a world city, just like Tokyo, New York or Berlin and the wonderful thing is the Parisians like to live in their city as if it were a village. It is true that Paris is a museum, or a city of the past, but there is a lot of living going on behind those monuments!"

"Children have this wonderful good mood and such an open mind. They are a permanent source of happiness and this is something we try to preserve."

# Beijing, China
## Nadia, Sundiata, Idris & Mira

China's massive capital, Beijing, has a history stretching back three millennia, however it's known as much for its modern architecture as it is for its ancient sites, such as the Forbidden City complex and the imperial palace from the Ming and Qing dynasties. With a population of almost 22 million people, Beijing recently made the world's stage, when it hosted the 2008 Summer Olympics. With plans to host the Winter Olympics in 2022, it will be the first and only city on the globe to host both events.

To the south of the central business district of Beijing is a suburb called Chaoyang, which is both close to the city's historic sites and near to expat neighbourhoods. Despite being so close to the city centre, there are still quiet and calm spaces, private compounds and the beautiful Qing Feng park just a short walk away. Chaoyang is also home to the Olympic Green (which was built for the 2008 Olympics) and is the most populous suburb in Beijing with over 3.5 million residents.

You could certainly call Nadia (who is half Persian), her husband, Sundiata (who is African American), and their two children, Idris and Mira, 'citizens of the world'. Having lived in many countries, Nadia admits a lot has surprised her – often in a positive way – about life in Beijing. At the same time, she also believes Beijing has been the most challenging place she's lived to date…and that's saying something! "I grew up in Swaziland, Cambodia, Thailand and the US," she explains. "The pollution, harsh winters and the language barrier here has definitely made adjusting to everyday life harder than other places that I've lived. That being said, the people are what make me love it here. When I think about the Chinese friends we have made – their purity, sincerity, gentle generosity

and, most of all, their love for children, stick out the most. I can't tell you how many times people have lovingly interacted with my children and offered anything to please them. You will never hear someone complain about a child crying or making a noise in a public place. Children are very much perceived as a blessing for all of society and they are treated with such gentle kindness and patience. It is so nice raising a young family in this environment. Beijing has also taught me never to take blue skies for granted. I never even thought much about blue skies before because they were such a norm. I will forever stop to appreciate them from now on and I thank Beijing for teaching me to value life's simple pleasures.

"I don't think that China is a country for everyone, but living here has taught us a lot about ourselves and made us realise that no matter where we move, we will adapt. One of the best things about living here is how safe we feel. For a city of more than 20 million people, crime is virtually non-existent, which is such a relief and removes so many barriers."

Nadia and Sundiata have been married for nine years and had always hoped to raise their family internationally. Nadia is a consultant in public health and international development allowing her to work for global organisations such as CARE, UNICEF and Save The Children. When Sundiata received the opportunity to teach at an international school in northeast China, they jumped at the opportunity. Having moved to Beijing and then welcoming their two children in the last three years has seen them settle in the city...well, sort of. "The rental market is on the rise here and landlords often sell their property quite quickly – meaning you often have to move at the drop of a hat! We love where we are now though. A colleague of my husbands once rented this apartment and when she decided to return to the US, she let us know it was available. It's so spacious and open compared to other apartments in the area and we knew right away we wanted to move in. Living internationally, you are conscious to not accumulate too much junk. When we first moved though, we realised how little we needed and we really only brought our favourite books, some paintings and some family portraits to make our apartment feel like 'home'. It does also help that Beijing doesn't have stores like Target, so accumulating lots of things is much less tempting. I do miss Target sometimes though!"

Even the children have taken on a multicultural view when it comes to their things and many of the family's favourites are items that have been discovered on travels over the years. "Since Idris was born three years ago we've been to South Africa, Hong Kong, Bali, Cambodia and the Philippines," Nadia says. "We love being able to travel with our kids and expose them to new cultures and other ways of life. Our home and their toys definitely reflect the myriad of cultures and people that live in this world. Most toys depict a very singular and Western way of life and that doesn't really resonate with the experiences that our kids have had here in China. Some of our favourite books and toys are from South Africa. We have a Desmond Tutu doll that my son loves and we bought a children's book written by Archbishop Desmond Tutu when we visited Cape Town titled, *God's Dream*. It talks about the beauty of the oneness of mankind which is a core tenet of our own beliefs."

The home this family has created is not just a place to keep the reminders of their travel adventures. Both the city they live in, and the age of the children, have impacted design decisions. "Because of the pollution here in Beijing, there are days when we have to stay inside all day long. I needed to make sure our home was safe (we have lots of air purifiers!), comfortable and engaging for the kids and any visitors. To me, that means making sure there is nothing on display that we would be sad to see broken or destroyed. We have lots of toys and books at toddler eye level and the kids have free reign in their playroom. This means lots of forts are built, big messes are made and there's enough space for family dancing at the end of the day when we are all getting cranky and tired!"

Nadia admits that part of the reason for wanting to raise their children in a different culture was an attempt to create balance in their lives and to really be able to appreciate family time. "We found our life in the US completely void of balance. We were working all the time and couldn't see how we could have a family in that context. Since leaving, we've been exposed to so many different families and we find their examples inspiring. Achieving balance is difficult, but taking a step back from the rat race allowed us time to reflect on the life that we want to live.

"My favourite time of the day is when all the family is home together. The time before dinner is reserved for family playtime – good music in the background and often a game of hide and seek! Having a family and living with kids means I am learning every moment of every day. Parenthood really is the most humbling experience. It's definitely the hardest, yet most important thing I've ever done and it's helped me grow in the most amazing way. I also think that getting to see the world through your child's new and unfiltered eyes is the most wondrous gift.

"Parenthood makes you so vulnerable. I never imagined the amount of love and hurt and raw vulnerability parenthood would bring. Watching your children experience struggle or life's tests – even in the smallest of terms – requires so much strength, humility and resilience. Sundiata and I joke all the time about how we will follow our children to college when they finally leave the house. They are the coolest people we know!"

*"In China, children are very much perceived as a blessing for all of society and as such they are treated with such gentle kindness and patience."*

# Toronto, Canada
## Amanda, Adam, Atticus & Archer

Toronto, the provincial capital of Ontario, Canada, is one the most culturally diverse cities on the planet. With over 140 languages spoken in Toronto, it is estimated over half of the city's 2.6 million residents were born outside of Canada. An international centre of business, finance, arts and culture, the city is recognised as one of the most multicultural and cosmopolitan in the world. After New York City, Los Angeles and Mexico City, Toronto is the fourth most populous city in North America. Despite its size and complex make-up, Torontonians generally get along and intolerance and race-related violence is uncommon.

With some of the world's finest restaurants, bars, clubs, galleries, sporting events and festivals as well as beautiful scenery along the shores of Lake Ontario, there is always something to enjoy in this vibrant city. Winters are long, white and cold but when the weather is warmer this is one place worth hitting the streets to explore.

Family of four — Adam, Amanda, Atticus and Archer ("we are the A-team!") — are based in Toronto but definitely consider the entire planet their home. "We're constantly curious," says Amanda of her globetrotting family. "We live for our family adventures — both locally and abroad."

The family's home is an apartment in central Toronto in a stunning old building filled with history and fascinating stories. "A friend of a friend lived in this building for years and I had fallen in love with her apartment after a short visit," explains Amanda. "Thanks to this connection, and my persistence — that pregnancy nesting instinct is strong — we made it through the board approval process seamlessly and when a rare unit became available, we jumped on the opportunity. It's an amazingly diverse community, with a mix of old school tenants who have been here for over 30 years, to some of Toronto's most notable politicians, actors and business owners. You can definitely feel the respect

that everyone has for the building and its rare energy, along with the gratitude we all share from the privilege of living here. The building and the apartment itself is such a beautiful, elegant throwback to a very different time.

"Adam and I have very similar tastes from a décor perspective. We both appreciate amazing architecture – both classic and contemporary. Our building is a relic from the 1930s that has been maintained by people who believe in honouring its history. There are few buildings remaining in the city that have their original floor plans intact. We love the large principle rooms, the beautiful mouldings, wood burning fireplaces and the small details like cedar-lined closets, storage, high ceilings and layout. It feels grand. Everyone who is lucky enough to live in this building seems to share our reverence for it."

Amanda says the moment they entered the apartment, she knew it was the perfect space for the family. "We moved in a few days after Atticus was born. I remember planning the move months earlier and making the naïve assumption that his birth would be late. My friends all said that first borns always arrive late! Of course, nothing ever goes to plan and our first month of parenting was quite unsettled as a result. We didn't even decorate the nursery or buy a crib until Atticus was almost six months old and we'd returned from our travels. We've now lived here for more than four years and whilst the neighbourhood wasn't new to us (Amanda and Adam lived just a few blocks away before their move), the way we experience the local services, amenities and shops has definitely evolved. I don't think I'd even really noticed any of the playgrounds that are now part of our daily itinerary."

Amanda is a lover and supporter of the arts – both locally and beyond – and the family home features many unique and special pieces that showcase her passion. "The décor in our home continues to evolve as we fall in and out of love with pieces of furniture and artwork we've collected or that we lust after. I think interior design is a process as opposed to a specific destination. There are some favourite pieces though. Our Huichol beaded skull is one. All of the intricate beadwork represents esoteric and sacred symbols. In the Huichol culture, art and religion are inextricable. Both of my parents spend most of the year in Mexico and, as a result, our little family feels a strong connection to Mexican culture that we wanted to celebrate in our home.

"Our artwork is all very personal and meaningful to me. Lots of photography. The most recent addition to our collection is a family portrait that was shot by LA photographer Gregg Segal as part of a waste awareness campaign we participated in (see page 106). The version hanging on our wall shows Archer nursing. It was captured as an outtake, but it was so beautiful and personal. A perfect moment in time that we would love to remember.

"It's been fun to build our home together, piece by piece. We've certainly amassed quite a collection of random tchotchkes, books, art and keepsakes from all our travels over the years. Now we also have two little people to take into account when making a home deco purchase."

Despite many beautiful pieces, Amanda says it's essential to her and Adam to let their children access every room in the house. "It was important to us that our home not become overrun with toys and plastic just because we had kids, however we didn't want it to be a museum either. We try to keep most things out of sight when they're not in use – cabinets, bins and baskets work well for us. No area of the house is off limits to the children. It's a comfortable, lived-in home and there is definitely something about the energy and space that makes it very welcoming.

"I think our home works well for adult-child play dates. When Atticus was little we started a tradition with some friends called Babies & Bubbly. Basically, it was an opportunity for us to be social on a Saturday afternoon without getting a sitter. Adult beverages are served and grown up conversations are on tap. The host makes snacks and an easy dinner for the kids so that when everyone heads home, the kids are fed and ready for bath and bed and mum and dad feel like they've had an evening out. We have lots of toys and long hallways for scooters and skateboards; a big, comfortable sectional in the living room and a large dining room that holds a big group.

"I love our home the most in the afternoon when Atticus and Archer are napping. It's usually my most productive time of day and the house feels so peaceful with the washing machine and dishwasher quietly chugging away. My heart melts when I see Atticus' messy little blonde head emerge and Archer's sleepy eyes trying to focus after he wakes... they are both such mama's boys and love a cuddle when they wake up. So that's what we do.

"Having children has definitely made our lives more significant. We're less selfish with our time and have shared goals and dreams versus personal ones. It's still amazing to think that these two little people are small parts of us and other pieces from our long family history. The discovery of who they are and guessing about who they'll become is a daily obsession and passion!"

With Adam travelling a lot for work, and Amanda working as a freelance travel writer alongside selling a gorgeous range of baby garments, the family is often on the move. "We try to join Adam whenever we can and, as an entrepreneur, I often have a packed schedule. Meeting with distributors or fabric suppliers whilst also carving out tons of time with the boys – museums, local parks and play dates. We also prioritise travelling as a family and try to spend time abroad to expose the boys to different cultures, cuisines and attitudes.

"We've been around the world and whenever we come back to Toronto we're reminded of just how much of an amazing place it is. It borrows the best of all cultures and harmonises them into something truly distinct. Canadians, on the whole, are also some of the friendliest, open and adventurous people so we always find interesting people and experiences. Now, if someone could just do something about our long winters..."

*To see more of Amanda and her family's life and travels go to www.theadventuresofatticus.tumblr.com and discover her beautiful range of baby garments on instagram (@petitsgenoux).*

*"We're constantly curious.
We live for our family adventures
- both locally and abroad."*

# Solana Beach, USA
## Noami, Benji, Matan & Ami

San Diego County is in the southwestern corner of the state of California. With 110km of beautiful coastline and a mild Mediterranean climate, the region was once part of Mexico, as is apparent by much of the older architecture in the area. A popular tourist destination, the county is enjoyed by surfers, hikers, golfers and shoppers alike.

Almost exactly halfway down San Diego County's coastline is a sweet little town called Solana Beach. With over 12,000 residents calling Solana Beach home, the town has over 85 art galleries, import and antique stores, boutiques and cafés along with the popular weekend Solana Beach Farmer's Market locally-grown fresh cut flowers and organic produce. The town is also known for its live music scene – the local club, Belly Up, having opened in 1974 and featuring international artists as well as popular cover bands.

Solana Beach is home to Noami and her family and she admits that, even while loving their nomadic life, they have embraced the wonder of their home and their town. "There are four of us on this adventure: my husband, Benji; Matan, the artist-athlete and Ami, the shot-calling-cuddlebug! Solana Beach is beautiful. I love that all the houses are so different and the fact that our kids can happily play outside and bike around like maniacs all day – we have nine kids under 10 in our cul-de-sac! You can easily walk to the lagoon, or the beach and we get so much sunshine. The cuteness is so thorough, it's almost sickening!" Noami laughs.

It wasn't the friendly street or the sunshiny days that won Noami and Benji over when it came to finding their home, though. It was the incredible backyard. "We snuck in one day and inhaled sharply when we saw the backyard," Noami says. "There were fruit trees we'd never even heard of! We knew we had to try for it. It was a six-month process, but it finally became ours."

The family knew they would need to make some changes inside the house to truly make it theirs, but they were also happy to live with the work-in-progress. "The house has a great, easy indoor/outdoor living area. We knew right away that we could work with it and we try to do one major

project a year with smaller changes ongoing. That keeps it manageable and still fun, but also makes us feel as though we are being productive."

Noami says their home is at its best first thing in the morning. "Dawn here is beautiful. The sunrise through our bedroom window is so many shades of spectacular. In the winter it looks as though the sky is on fire and the light is so pretty when the tangle-haired little guys wander out to have their breakfast and draw in the dining room."

"We love our little house because it means we are together when we are all home. Our living space spills out into the front and back yards and we can harvest fruit for snacks or smoothies… the macadamia nuts also make great projects of every kind and the strawberry guavas make the yummiest margaritas!"

Noami admits that living with kids has its challenges, especially when your home isn't huge. "Our house is small so the kids'' stuff' is certainly an issue for us. We don't want a ton of toys to whack people in the face as soon as they walk in the door. We have to be pretty creative when it comes to storage options – hollow stools, baskets and organised drawers all help – and we also try to filter through everything semi-regularly and get rid of as much stuff as possible. We have tried to be strict about the quality of materials we let in for our kids to play with, but birthday parties, grandparents and hand-me-downs have taught us to be more flexible and we understand that kids don't always want to play with the stationary wooden toy that adults find design-y or beautiful."

Noami's attitude of loving things for all the right reasons is apparent when she talks about her favourite items in the home: the Naftali Bezem painting ("We got it in Jaffa when I was pregnant, it's the most delicious illustration."); the Native American wedding vase ("It was a gift and it always tips merrily on the dresser but never quite falls over."); the waterfall bedroom set ("We found it in LA, got a stranger to deliver it through taskrabbit and distributed it through different rooms in the house."); the dreamcatcher above Ami's crib ("made from things Matan found, including a palm part that looks like a bull!"); and the type drawer treasure display ("the kids always have their eye out for heart shaped rocks") but most of all she loves her books. "We have bookshelves everywhere and there's something about having artwork and lots of books in your home that makes everything in life seem more accessible."

With Noami working as VP for a non-profit organisation that develops affordable housing throughout California, and Benji having a boutique real estate investment company, the family keep very busy. "We have done several projects together," Noami explains. "The kids have been on many construction sites! They've ridden in forklifts, painted and helped with layouts but we try to tuck away time to laugh as adults too. Benji and I try for yoga dates or beach walk dates or wine, but mostly we include the kids in the things we do. There never seems to be enough hours in the day. We push ourselves to be efficient and productive so we can spend time more freely, but we still have a long list of things we'd like to get done."

For now though, Noami and Benji are trying to enjoy the little things. "There's lots to love. The cuddles, the laughter and the learning together. Meal times, cooking together and every single detail of how they smell when they wake up in the morning. We try to honour whatever they are into in any phase – paper aeroplanes, asteroids, Hamilton, and explore them together as a family. Everything can become an adventure or a dance party! And the words they make up - we all end up using them – everyone in our family now calls a sweet treat "booma" because that's the word Ami uses."

Noami and Benji love to travel and now there are two children along for the ride, Noami admits she's become quite the master at finding tiny little games or objects that will keep the kids amused when they're out and about. "Always take pen and paper. . .and snacks!  Lots of snacks," she laughs.

"In a way though, our little beach community of Solana Beach includes so many of the things that we love about our favourite places around the world – walking to the beach, great restaurants, fabulous music venues, parks and shops. We just love it here."

"There never seems to be enough hours in the day. We push ourselves to be more efficient and more productive so we can spend time more freely."

# About Kid & Coe

Kid & Coe's founder, Zoie Kingsbery Coe, created Kid & Coe out of necessity. For years she had been traveling the world managing her husband's music career and then, with kids in tow, she found the hotels that once suited a touring couple no longer fit the needs of her growing family. Zoie began to seek out kid-friendly property rentals that made her family feel at home wherever they were in the world. An increasing number of parents asked Zoie to share her secrets and so Kid & Coe was born. The US-based company was established in 2013 and currently offers over 700 properties in six continents with more being added every week. The team at Kid & Coe are their own audience and understand what makes family travel irresistible yet tricky.

Zoie, her husband and their two children now split their time between New York, London, Ibiza and Los Angeles.

All of the family homes featured in this book are available to rent for short-term holidays via **www.kidandcoe.com**

# Mi Casa Es Su Casa

**All of our homeowners generously open up their homes to share with other families. Many of them said that they welcome the opportunity to take a little holiday during the time their home is being shared, and they all said they love giving other families the opportunity to enjoy their home cities and towns. I was keen to know how they really feel about letting other families live in their space...**

"We can't be there all the time and it's such a shame to let a beautiful place be empty. We want people to enjoy the space, explore the area, appreciate the house and the area that we have chosen to have a home. It's a haven to escape to from our busy lives."

- Christina, Andalucía (Spain)

"When we travel we like to rent apartments, so in a way we have always gone into the home of strangers. We find this both a natural and exciting way to travel. As long as there is a garden, some books or toys or a musical instrument the children find their fun and feel good. In return, we try to prepare our apartment in a way that each family visiting will enjoy it – flowers, a guide book, new soap. It's the little things."

- Irene, Vienna (Austria)

"We remove some personal belongings but not all of them – we don't want to make the home impersonal as it takes away from the experience of those staying. Yes, they are strangers, but they have felt a connection with our home and that's why they've chosen it. That gives life to our home... an additional soul. We love to welcome people to our place and share the comforts that we have."

- Margarida, Alentejo (Portugal)

"We definitely do our research on people who want to stay in our home and make sure we are 100 per cent comfortable with them. We've found it really easy though and haven't had any challenges."

- Hayley, Melbourne (Australia)

"Some people couldn't share their home – they might see it as an intrusion on their space – but not us, that's not our way of thinking. We are really glad when others have a good time in our home. It's like preparing a wonderful dinner for your friends."

- Benjamin, Paris (France)

"We love sharing our home with strangers! Nothing is so precious that we would care if it were broken or damaged though and I think that helps a lot."

- Nadia, Beijing (China)

# Photo Credits

Cover image: **João Morgado**

Page 1: **Nadia Shadravan**

Pages 4 & 5: (Watercolour World Map) **Pavlo Raievskyi**

Page 6: **Yoon Kim**

Page 7: **Kid & Coe**

Page 8: (Family image) **Margarida Adonis**

Pages 9, 10, 11, 12, 13, 14, 15: (Casa Do Óc Residence – Alentejo, Portugal) **João Morgado**

Page 16: (Family image) **Loïca Bonini**

Pages 17, 18, 19, 20, 21, 22, 23: (Saint Gabriel Residence – Provence, France) **Kid & Coe**

Page 24: (Family image) **Philip Waddler**

Pages 25, 26, 27, 28, 29, 30, 31, 32, 33: (Mangaba Residence – Boipeba, Brazil) **Marcelo Reis**

Page 34: (Family image) **Irene Yerro**

Pages 35, 36, 37, 38, 39, 40, 41: (Gumpendorfer Residence – Austria, Vienna) **Maurizio Meier**

Page 42: (Family image) **Kate Di Blasi**

Pages 43, 44, 45, 46, 47, 48, 49: (Mackay Residence – Melbourne, Australia) **Chris Underwood**

Page 50: (Family image) **Jami Saunders**

Pages 51, 52, 53, 54, 55, 56, 57: (N. 8th Street Residence – Williamsburg, USA) **Yoon Kim**

Pages 58, 59, 60, 61, 62, 63, 64, 65: (Maynard Street Residence - Cape Town, South Africa) **Marli du Toit**

Pages 66, 69, 70, 72, 73: (Bernadottesgatan Residence – Malmö, Sweden) **Peter Brandshøj**

Pages 67, 68, 70, 71: (Bernadottesgatan Residence – Malmö, Sweden) **Markus Linderoth**

Pages 74, 75, 76, 77, 78, 79, 80, 81: (Vejer Residence – Andalucía, Spain) **Christina Wilson**

Page 82: (Family image) **Elizabeth Harris**

Pages 83, 84, 85, 86, 87, 88, 89: (Cambridge Street Residence – Sydney, Australia) **Jacqui Turk**

Pages 90, 91, 93, 94, 95, 96: (Cesar Residence – Paris, France) **Benjamin Lalande**

Pages 92, 97: (Cesar Residence – Paris, France) **Kid & Coe**

Pages 98, 99, 100, 101, 102, 103, 104, 105: (Shiqiao Guomao Residence – Beijing, China) **Nadia Shadravan**

Page 106: (Family image) **Gregg Segal**

Pages 107, 108, 109, 110, 111, 112, 113: (Clarendon Avenue Residence - Toronto, Canada) **Mirza Noormohamad**

Page 114: (Family image) **Noami Pines**

Pages 115, 116, 117, 118, 119, 120, 121: (Ridgeline Place Residence – Solana Beach, USA) **Rancho Photos**

Page 122: **Davina Zagury**

Page 125: **Mirza Noormohamad**

# Acknowledgements

A very special thank you to all the people who worked hard helping to create this lovely book...

All of the wonderful families who shared their images and their stories, but who also continue to share their homes each day through Kid & Coe

Lauren Mitchell for her editing skills
Dave Lowther for his design savvy
Cheree Heath, Mel Lowther and Helen Morgan for their advice and feedback
And to Rod, Oscar and Sebastian for being so awesome (and for sharing my love of the world)

Finally, an extra, extra huge thanks to Laura Hall for not only making this book happen but for all her hard work, co-ordination and wonderful advice along the way!

www.ingramcontent.com/pod-product-compliance
Lightning Source LLC
Chambersburg PA
CBHW040335300426
44113CB00021B/2757